In memory of my Mother, Bee Bartholomew, who lives in my heart and who's strength I've become. Mom was a wonderful mother, wife and grandmother (Nana) who touched many lives.

Special Memories of Nana

Many Blessings to your family! Jane K.

by **Jane M. Kritzman**

illustrated by **Kristy Stadleburger**

Hello.
My name is
Kathryn,
and this is
my Nana.

This is where my Nana lives.

It's fun to go visit with her.

Nana has
a funny smile,
her hands are
soft and her
hugs make me
warm.

On Sunday mornings we pick Nana up in the car. We all go to church.

Nana and I like to sing and pray in church.

After church we go to Nana's house to visit.

Many times Nana makes dinner for us at her house.

She puts on her special apron and even lets me help!

Nana is a very good cook!

My favorite dinner is Nana's pork roast and her homemade apple pie.

It's very delicious!

Nana loves to sew and sometimes I get to help her!

I cut squares of fabric, and Nana carefully sewed them together. When it was all put together, it made a beautiful quilt.

I was so surprised when Nana gave it to me to bring home for my very own bed!

One day, Nana's heart hurt.

She had to take a ride in an ambulance to the hospital.

Even Nana had to wear the funny pajamas in the hospital.

Nana was tired and so sick. Mommy went to visit Nana at the hospital.

When Mommy came home she was very sad.

She said that Nana went to heaven.

Mommy and I, and all of Nana's friends went to the church. It was a funeral for Nana.

People were saying nice things about my Nana. They prayed for her.

Nana may be in heaven, but I remember her, and smile and say a prayer.

Now Mommy wears Nana's apron when she cooks apple pie and I think of Nana.

It makes me happy so I smile!

Mommy asks me why I'm smiling.

I know my heart is happy when I think of Nana, so I put my hand over my heart and I tell her –

Because Mommy, my special memories of Nana are still in here!

I climbed in my bed and my mommy tucked me in.

I remembered Nana when I snuggled in the quilt she sewed for me.

It was like one of her hugs, warm and loving, and I fell fast asleep.